# ingrid michaelson
## *human again*

This book was approved by Ingrid Michaelson

Cover painting by Joe Sorren

Piano/vocal arrangements by John Nicholas

Cherry Lane Music Company
Director of Publications/Project Editor: Mark Phillips

ISBN 978-1-60378-443-6

*Visit our website at www.cherrylaneprint.com*

# ingrid michaelson
## *human again*

When she walks into a store in her Brooklyn neighborhood, Ingrid Michaelson is rarely recognized. But once she hands over her credit card to pay, the clerk often pauses, brightens up, and enthusiastically offers a bit of trivia: "Did you know that there's a singer named Ingrid Michaelson?"

Image has never been her priority, but Michaelson has earned enviable name-recognition thanks to her knack for crafting beautiful, idiosyncratic songs such as "The Way I Am," "Maybe," and "Keep Breathing." And let the record show that her librarian-chic style has nonetheless received a shout-out in *The New York Times*.

Michaelson's grassroots sensibility has worked like gangbusters: Her music, often about love and relationships, has wafted out of your television in handfuls of *Grey's Anatomy* episodes (not to mention countless other series since, such as *American Idol*, *Parenthood*, and *So You Think You Can Dance*), in an affecting Google Chrome ad, and on VH1 as an artist You Outta Know. *The New York Times* marveled that she was "singing her way from obscurity to fame." *Billboard* trumpeted her as the face of the new music business. NPR declared, "Ingrid Michaelson is everywhere." As an independent artist she has sold over 750,000 albums and 3,000,000 singles.

With *Human Again*, produced by David Kahne (Regina Spektor, Paul McCartney), Michaelson throws a wrench in her reputation as the Crafter of Dainty Love Songs. "The album is called *Human Again*, because it's taken me a very long time to be happy," she says. "I am writing about a really dark time in my life even though I'm not there." One of her most gutting compositions is *Human*'s first single, "Ghost," a hushed reflection on lost romance that unfurls ruefully from its opening line, "Do you remember when the walls fell?" From there, Michaelson plumbs the breadth of human emotion. The feisty "Blood Brothers," in contrast, is a buoyant pop tune that actually "came from a place of annoyance," she says. "Like you're walking down the street, and someone shoulder-checks you while they're rushing by. Wouldn't it be nice if we treated each other like companions? Come on, everybody—stop being assholes!"

*Human Again* is also a triumph in aural range. The music veers from orchestral (Kahne's specialty) to percussive, while Michaelson's accompanying voice swells from contralto to soprano. "I think I was really singing out, physically, on this album," she says. "Usually that's set aside for divas, and the rest of us kind of have to whisper and be precious. I figured, 'Why don't I just put that out on at least one record in my career—let it all hang out?' " No track better captures the alternating thoughtfulness and unrest of *Human Again* than "Fire," a string-laden anthem in which she sings about an emotional slash-and-burn: "I will grow from the ground after you burn me down." Notes Michaelson, "That is kind of a thread that runs throughout the record."

Such artistic ambition has always percolated in the blood of this singer-songwriter—who's also co-written and starred in a semi-autobiographical, comedic pilot that she and improv-actress Rebekka Johnson are shopping around to TV networks. (The show is still untitled.) The Staten Island–raised daughter of classical music composer Carl Michaelson, she took piano lessons from the age of five and starred in plays during her grade school years. Michaelson went on to study musical theater at Binghamton University in upstate New York, where she sang in an a cappella group. After graduating, she cultivated her interest in music by performing at a coffee house, where she worked as a barista. She was teaching theater to kids when she got a fateful call in 2006 from a music manager named Lynn Grossman whose company Secret Road discovered Michaelson's homegrown tunes on her MySpace page.

Within a few months, Michaelson's music could be found sound-tracking the romantic-surgical debauchery *Grey's Anatomy* with such songs as the cascading "Breakable" and the melancholic lullaby "Keep Breathing." A music supervisor for Old Navy just happened to catch the episode featuring the latter and snapped up the cooing, calypso-inflected "The Way I Am" for one of the company's commercials. (The song ultimately went platinum.) Radio play followed, just in time for the release of her 2007 full-length debut, *Girls and Boys* (out on Cabin 24 Records, her own imprint). This all happened in about a year. "We really had a lot of luck, and then we worked really hard to be in the position we're in nowadays," says Michaelson, who's since released an EP, 2008's *Be OK*, and a follow-up album, *Everybody* (both via the Cabin 24 label)—each proving fertile resources for music licensors.

*Human Again* expands on Michaelson's melodic roots. And it's an ambitious move for her, one that's even surprised her parents. "My father said, 'Where are all the ditties?' " she recalls, laughing. "I said, 'Well, I think I'm past the ditties, Dad.' I'm done with that part of my life. I'm ready to think a little bolder."

# Fire

Words and Music by
Ingrid Michaelson

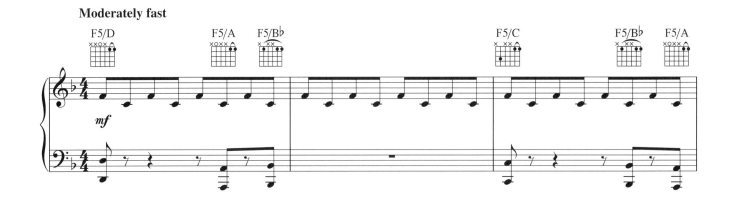

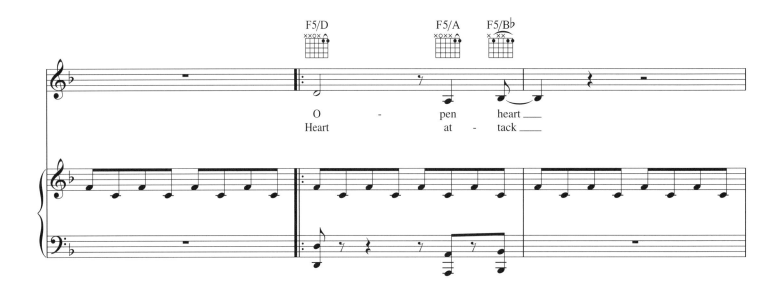

O - pen heart ___
Heart at - tack ___

sur - ger - y; ___ that is what ___
up your sleeve. ___ You can make ___

ing in a fi - re when I walk __ in - to you, __ in - to you, __ __ in - to you, __ in - to you, __ in - to you, __ in - to you. __ (In - to you, __ in - to you, __ __ in - to you.) __ In - to you, __ __ in - to you, __ in - to you. __

# This Is War

Words and Music by
Ingrid Michaelson

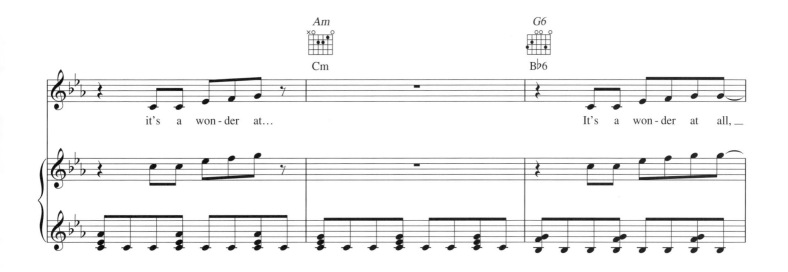

You lock __ me out. __

You knock __ me down. __ But I ____ will find ____ my way a - round. __

__ I won't __ sur - ren - der. __

This is war. __

# Do It Now

Words and Music by
Ingrid Michaelson

Sit - ting in the back of the bus, ___ talk - in' a - bout noth - in'. Oh, we're talk - in' 'bout us, ___ watch - ing as the world goes ___ ham - mer - ing on, ___ ham - mer - ing ___ on. _____

No one's gon - na wait for you. ____ So do it now. ____

Do it right ____ now. ____ Don't waste a min - ute on the

dark - ness and the pit - y sit - ting in your mind, and do it right now, ____

and do it right now. ____

of my bed. You're gon-na stand __ up. You're __ gon-na stand __ up.

You're gon-na stand __ up. _____ You're gon-na stand __ up. _____

*D.S.S. al Coda II*

So

Coda II

now. _____ Do it right

now.

(Now. _____ Do it right now.)

# I'm Through

Words and Music by
Ingrid Michaelson

# Blood Brothers

Words and Music by
Ingrid Michaelson

# Black and Blue

Words and Music by
Ingrid Michaelson

black and blue ___ and in love ____ with you. ___ You said you
Black and blue, in love with you. You said...

nev - er would let me fall, you nev - er would let me fall, ___ but I'm fall - ing. You
...let me fall. You said... But I'm fall - ing.

*To Coda*

nev - er would let me fall, you nev - er would let me fall, ___ but I'm fall - ing.
...let me fall. You said... But I'm fall - ing.)

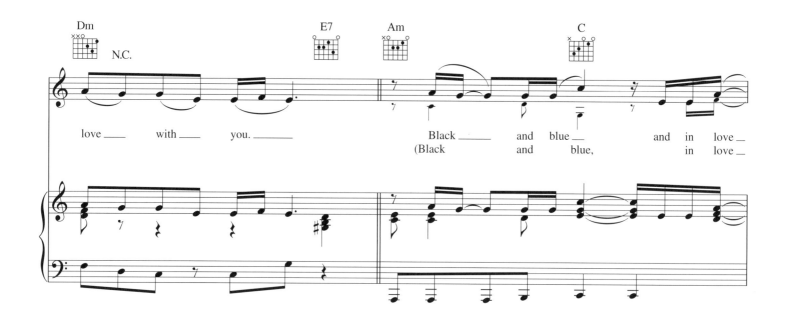

love ___ with ___ you. ___     Black ___ and blue ___     and in love ___
(Black     and blue,     in love ___

___ with you. ___ You said     you nev - er would let me fall, ___ you
___ with you. You said…     …let me fall.

nev - er would let me fall, ___ but I'm fall - ing. You nev - er would let me fall, ___ you
But I'm fall - ing.     …let me fall. You said…

# Ribbons

Words and Music by
Ingrid Michaelson

Moderately fast

I'm sit-ting pret-ty and I don't know why. __ I __ found some-bod-y, said he'd make me fly. __ Wrapped __ me up in rib-bons, then he left me to die. __ Wrapped __ me up in rib-bons, then he left me to die. __

Told me he'd hold me 'til there was no more. __ Told __ me that he'd love me from the top to the floor. __ Wrapped __ me up in rib-bons, then he went for the door. __ Wrapped __ me up in rib-bons, then he

*Recorded a half step lower.

44

You look so pret-ty in the dark of night, __ but __ I'm get-ting wise in the
You put your Sun-day best on for us all, __ paint-ing up a prom-ise that you

ear-ly light. __ I ____ can see you fall-ing like a home-made kite. __ I ____
know will fall. __ Wrap __ me in your rib-bons, tie me to the wall. __ Wrap __

____ can see you fall-ing like a home-made kite. __ to the wall. __ And
____ me in your rib-bons, tie me

*D.S. al Coda*

# How We Love

Words and Music by
Ingrid Michaelson

*Guitarists: Use open E tuning (low to high): E-B-E-G♯-B-E.

girl came by; she had eyes ___ like the ris - ing tide. ___
win - ter clove and sparked like fire - wood in - side ___ a stove. ___

He felt a sharp - ness deep in - side, ___ the kind of ache that can't be
Want - ed to ask her just to sit and stay; ___ in - stead, he watched as she

sat - is - fied. }
walked a - way. } We ___ hate the rain ___ when it fills ___

___ up our shoes, ___ but ___ how we love ___ when it wash - es our cars. ___

# Palm of Your Hand

Words and Music by
Ingrid Michaelson

*Guitarists: Tune down a half step (low to high): E♭-A♭-D♭-G♭-B♭-E♭.

# Ghost

Words and Music by
Ingrid Michaelson

# In the Sea

Words and Music by
Ingrid Michaelson

*Recorded a half step lower.

**Chords implied by bass.

# Keep Warm

Words and Music by
Ingrid Michaelson

Eyes ___ on the prize ___ and I can't ___ cap - size this time 'cause

there's some - bod - y else in my boat. ___

Used ___ to live a - lone ___ in a tomb I made ___ my own, ___ but

cold out - side ____ but I'm just fine. ____ You are mine ___ to keep

warm. _____ Yeah, it's warm. _____

Sa - bles and wine till the end of time. ____ Oh, ____ you

give me much more _____ than __ that. __ Dia - mond rings and

# End of the World

Words and Music by
Ingrid Michaelson

# More Great Piano/Vocal Books

## FROM CHERRY LANE

For a complete listing of Cherry Lane titles available,
including contents listings, please visit our web site at
**www.cherrylane.com**

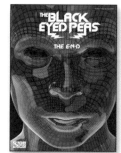